20 Best

Florida Beaches

and

Coastal Cities

A look at the history, highlights and things to do in some of Florida's best beaches and coastal cities

Gillian Birch

Gillian Birch

Cover Photo: Miami Beach

ISBN-13: 978-1505239881

ISBN-10: 1505239883

To Jamie, Pam, Daniel and Joseph

For all the joy you give

1. Amelia Island
2. St Augustine
3. Daytona Beach
4. Cocoa Beach
5. Palm Beach
6. Boca Raton
7. Fort Lauderdale
8. Miami Beach
9. Key Biscayne
10. Key West
11. Naples
12. Fort Myers
13. Venice
14. St Pete Beach
15. Tampa
16. Tarpon Springs
17. Cedar Key
18. Cape San Blas
19. Destin
20. Pensacola

©G. Birch

CONTENTS

Gillian Birch

Preface

The state of Florida has the longest coastline in the contiguous United States, stretching for 1,350 miles or 2,170 km. This gives visitors an endless number of beaches to choose from along both the Atlantic Ocean seaboard and the Gulf of Mexico. *20 Best Florida Beaches and Coastal Cities* covers the entire state, highlighting the best beaches to help visitors and residents find the most ideal beach to suit their requirements. Each chapter highlights a specific coastal city and gives a brief historic note along with a colorful description, gorgeous photographs and a comprehensive list of things to do.

Low lying and marshy, Florida was only significantly developed with the arrival of the first railroad from Fernandina Beach to Cedar Key in the 1860s, hence most cities are less than 150 years old. The majority were primarily developed around the coastline. After the Civil War and the building of the Florida East Coast Railroad by Henry Flagler in 1885, the benefits of developing Florida as a winter haven quickly became apparent.

With a tropical climate, Florida continues to be popular all year round for visitors, but especially in the winter months when it is pleasantly warm and dry. Visitors from the northern states, Canada and northern Europe flock to Florida's beaches and coastal cities for a reprieve from the icy blasts and winter storms that prevail elsewhere.

From Amelia Island to the Florida Keys, Florida offers some wonderful beaches and the state's history is closely entwined with its coastal geology. Some beaches have powder-soft white sand such as Fort Myers Beach, which is absolutely perfect for building sandcastles, and that's official, as it hosts the World Championships of Sandsculpting every year. On the opposite coast, the firm sand at Daytona Beach packed by the relentless Atlantic breakers led to the developing of the unofficial racetrack for early motor racing.

20 Best Florida Beaches and Coastal Cities circumnavigates the Sunshine State, starting in the far northeastern tip, running down the Atlantic coast, around the Straits of Florida and up the Gulf Coast before heading west along the Panhandle where yet more beautiful beaches lie in store.

Along the way, discover the history, development and unique features that make each coastal city what it is today. Learn about St Augustine, the oldest continuously inhabited city in the U.S. with its fortified castle, and Tarpon Springs, a transplanted Greek community that still has a sponge-diving industry. The coastal city of Tarpon Springs continues to delight visitors with its delicious *baklava* bakeries, colorful waterfront and a Greek Orthodox Church modeled on St Sophia Church in Istanbul.

Whether you are looking for a Florida city to relocate to, researching your next vacation destination in Florida or simply want an informative read from your armchair, *20 Best Florida Beaches and Coastal Cities* presents interesting and informative facts with eyewitness detail about some of Florida's most charming destinations. Of course, there were many more worthy contenders that will have to wait for another volume!

Written in an informative style by a resident Florida travel writer, this book sets out to entertain, inform and inspire visitors to travel to Florida and take their pick of these delightfully unspoiled places.

Happy Trails!

20 Best

Florida Beaches

and

Coastal Cities:

A look at the history, highlights and things to do in some of Florida's best beaches and coastal cities

Gillian Birch

Beautiful Amelia Island

Exclusive Amelia Island is just 30 miles northeast of Jacksonville in northeast Florida. It is easy to reach by car across either Heckscher Bridge or the Ocean Blvd Bridge. This barrier island is well known for its beautiful sandy beaches, quaint town and interesting history. It was recently voted one of the Top North American Islands by Condé Nast Traveler.

Amelia Island

Amelia Island was nicknamed the "Isle of Eight Flags" as it has been claimed by so many different nations. Following the Timucuan Indians, the island belonged to France, then Spain, England, the "Patriots" of Amelia Island, the Republic of Florida, Mexico, the United States and the Confederacy, so it has quite a mixed history of cultures.

The main and only town on Amelia Island is Fernandina Beach. As an important seaport with the deepest natural harbor in the south, it now has a charming historic district left behind in a time warp with a wonderful legacy of architecture. Its Queen Anne, Victorian and Italianate mansions were once the winter homes of some of America's wealthiest families such as the Pulitzers and the Goodyears.

Cobbled Centre Street is a pleasing collection of Victorian buildings, now housing art galleries, restaurants, B&Bs and small shops selling gifts and whimsy. The Palace Saloon, one of many buildings on the National Register of Historic Places, claims the prize for being Florida's oldest continuously operating bar.

Things to Do on Amelia Island

The Museum of History prefers to relate history through storytelling. Knowledgeable docents lead a variety of informative walking tours on topics as varied as "The Golden Era of Amelia Island" and "The Seas of Change: the Story of Nassau County".

If you really want a feel of what Florida was like in the 1800s, a trip to Fort Clinch State Park should not be missed. The well-preserved fort complex, complete with cannons, was part of Civil War history and troops were garrisoned there, although they never saw any action.

The island has 13 miles of enviable beaches, miles of bike trails, dozens of tennis courts, six golf courses including the 18-hole PGA championship golf course at the grand Ritz-Carlton, and even its own nature center at the Amelia Island Plantation.

Visitors flock to the island on the first weekend in May for the Eight Flags Shrimp Festival when trays galore of fresh shrimps and seafood are consumed, accompanied by live music and fireworks. Other annual events are the Amelia Island Jazz Festival, the Chamber Music Festival, Amelia Island Film Festival and the Blues Festival. During the Concours d'Elegance the area is inundated with rare and elegant vintage cars, making the town look just as it did at the turn of the century. It is considered one of the premier concours events in the world.

Like many high end resorts in Florida, Amelia Island has some excellent restaurants for discerning gourmets looking for southern hospitality. From afternoon tea on the lawn of Hoyt House to the aviation themed Falcon's Nest at the Omni, you will certainly not go hungry on Amelia Island.

St Augustine - America's Oldest European Settlement

Many people complain that Florida has no real history. It's true, it doesn't have much compared to Europe, but the history it does have is very impressive. For example, did you know that America's oldest continuously occupied settlement is St Augustine in Florida?

The city was founded in 1565 by Pedro Menendez de Aviles on the feast day of St Augustine, hence how the city got its name. In 1702, the city burnt down and was rebuilt in the shadow of the huge Castillo de San Marcus. Many of these 300-year old buildings can still be seen today, lining the narrow pretty streets of the old town.

In 1883, railroad magnate Henry Flagler visited St Augustine on his honeymoon. He was so impressed with the area's potential as a winter playground for the rich, he returned again and built several hotels including the grand Spanish Renaissance style Ponce de Leon Hotel. This was the first-ever poured concrete building in the USA, completed in 1888, and it was one of the first buildings in the city to have electricity. This National Historic Landmark is now occupied by Flagler College. Visitors began to follow his example and soon St Augustine became a popular tourist destination, as it continues to be today.

Things to Do in St Augustine

Modern-day visitors will find St Augustine is a charming and unique town with beautiful buildings, interesting attractions and a fascinating historic district. It is a compact city, easy to walk around with plenty of lovely cafés and high-end restaurants. Trolley tours are a great way to enjoy an informative look at the main historic sites with an informative guide. Take a ghost tour of the city or visit the incredible Ripley's Believe It or Not! attraction nearby.

Stroll to the old Castillo de San Marco, overlooking the Intracoastal Waterway which is spanned by the Bridge of Lions. Enter the Old City Gate and wander along the cobblestone streets to the Plaza de la Constitution. St George Street is a traffic-free area with a collection of historic buildings, cafés and small shops selling ice cream, chocolates, gifts and antiques.

Explore the Colonial Spanish Quarter with its charming higgledy-piggledy buildings including America's oldest wooden schoolhouse. A massive chain encircles this cypress and red cedar building and anchors it to the ground during high winds! Other interesting attractions include the Spanish Quarter Museum that has seven reconstructed buildings with costumed interpreters demonstrating crafts and skills from the mid-18th century.

King Street, St Augustine

In contrast, King Street is the heart of the more modern city. Lined with beautiful Spanish-influenced architecture, it is very pleasant to stroll along and admire the buildings such as Government House with its Spanish-style loggias. The Hispanic-Moorish building that was once the Alcazar Hotel now houses the impressive Tiffany glass and antiques of the Lightner Museum collection.

Further west along King Street you will find Villa Zorayda with its Arabic motifs, a replica of the fabulous Alhambra Palace in Granada, Spain and further along is the well-known San Sebastian Winery.

There are several beaches around St Augustine including the white sands of Anastasia Island Beach, just five minutes from downtown. It has a pier, playground, pavilion, cafés and shops. Crescent Beach is also on Anastasia Island, a wildlife refuge with a natural setting that is popular for beachcombing. Vilano Beach is said to be the area's best kept secret with waterfront restaurants, a fishing pier, parasailing and SeaDoo rentals.

Daytona Beach and the International Speedway

Daytona Beach is an endless stretch of sand running down the Atlantic coast of Florida, south of Jacksonville and St Augustine, and just north of New Smyrna Beach. It is about 90 minutes' drive from Orlando along the I-4 and makes a great day out for those wanting to visit the beach from Orlando or Kissimmee.

The city of Daytona Beach is a sizeable community with a marina, the Volusia Mall and Daytona International Speedway. There are plenty of places to eat and all the usual small businesses you will find in any Florida community, from tire shops to real estate agencies, banks, liquor stores, fast food restaurants, Starbucks, Seven-Eleven stores, Wal-Mart, Sams Club and Walgreens. If you need anything, you will find it in Daytona Beach!

Ocean Walk Village, Daytona Beach

One of the most modern entertainment areas is at the end of Main Street and is known as the Ocean Walk Village. The complex has several upmarket hotels and a theater, shops, amusements, oceanfront dining, bars and restaurants.

A particular favorite is the Hyde Park Steakhouse Restaurant in the Hilton Hotel where you can get great deals on cocktails from 5pm with small plates of lite bites and superb steaks with excellent side dishes. It is an upmarket restaurant but the deals and early bird specials make it a great value place to dine with topnotch waiter service.

Right across the street from Ocean Walk Village is the Convention Center and the Daytona Lagoon Waterpark and Arcade. Nearby is a children's playground, fun center, boardwalk and the pier.

Daytona Beach itself has firmly packed sand and rolling waves making it ideal for surfing, kite-surfing or long walks in the constant breeze. Even on the hottest day, the beach is bearable if you have some shade from an umbrella and an onshore wind. There are sunbeds and umbrellas for hire near the hotels. High-rise apartment buildings are often shuttered against hurricanes as their owners visit for just a few weeks each year. The more popular buildings tend to be timeshare-owned with lovely swimming pools and beach bars.

There are some amusement parks and rides along the beach in places but as you travel further south the beach becomes quieter and is overlooked by private beach houses of all sizes and ages. The best thing about Daytona Beach is that for around $6 you can drive your car onto the beach and park for the day. Vans patrol up and down selling drinks and snacks and there are lifeguards at the most popular locations.

Things to Do in Daytona Beach

There are plenty of things to do around Daytona Beach apart from the beach and shops. Take a relaxing trip on the Halifax River to see the dolphins, birds and wildlife. In the winter, the St John's River is where many manatees gather to feed.

Alternatively, take the Daytona Trolley Bus Tour around the sights or enjoy a tour in one of the amphibious vehicles that start on the highway and then plunge into the river. The Museum of Photography and the Ormond Memorial Art Museum are also worth paying a visit.

Daytona International Speedway – the World Center of Racing

It was the miles of firm sand on Daytona Beach that gave birth to it becoming the home of supercharged speed. The first Daytona Speedway races ran for almost 50 years on an unofficial racing circuit that included the beach and part of the A1A Highway which runs parallel.

Finally the racing was placed on a more permanent footing when the Daytona International Speedway was built in 1959 on what became known as International Speedway Drive. The stadium has since become a landmark of the area. The track is 2½ miles long and the building of the improved circuit coincided with faster and more reliable racing cars, so the main race was increased from 200 to 500 miles in length.

Daytona 500

The Daytona 500 is NASCAR's biggest and most prestigious event on the racing calendar and usually takes place on the last Sunday in February each year. The event involves around 40 of the best stock car drivers and 2013 is the 55th annual event. The race is 500 miles long, which is 200 laps, and is the first series race of the year. Its importance in the racing calendar has led to it being called the "Super Bowl of Stock Car Racing".

The Daytona 500 draws around 200,000 visitors to Daytona every year to watch this exciting event live. The winner is presented with the Harley J. Earl Trophy in Victory Lane and the winning car is displayed at the Speedway Museum dedicated to the Daytona 500 Experience.

Daytona International Speedway

Other Events at the Daytona Speedway

If you cannot get to Daytona in February to see the Daytona 500, there are plenty more races and events throughout the year including the Rolex 24, the Budweiser Shootout for the NASCAR Sprint Cup, the Coke Zero 400 and a host of motorcycle events.

When races are not in progress visitors can take a guided tour of the huge stadium on the 480-acre site. Guides take you behind the scenes to see what is involved in making NASCAR events run so smoothly. Visitors get to see the Drivers' Meeting Room, tour the NASCAR Spring Cup Series garages, view the Victory Lane and take a peek inside the press box, seven floors above the track itself. Full tours cost around $22 for adults. There are other shorter and cheaper tours available giving visitors access to the NASCAR Nationwide Series garages, pit and the infield.

Cocoa Beach – Orlando's Local Beach

For millions of visitors to Florida every year, their first visit is usually to Orlando and the highlight is often spending a few days at Cocoa Beach on the Atlantic Coast. The endless sands, warm waters and lack of crowds makes this one of Florida's most popular beaches.

Cocoa Beach is home to around 12,500 residents and many more thousands of visitors pass through every year. It is located just south of Cape Canaveral near Merritt Island. Cocoa Beach is known as the "Small-Wave Capital of the World". It is ideal for beginner surfing with predictable rolling surf. Once you have mastered your balance, it is the perfect place to show off your moves, as many wetsuit-clad surfers do by the pier.

Close by is the world-famous Ron Jon Surf Shop – open 24/7 with everything you can possibly imagine for rent or for sale in the Art Deco Surf Palace. It is the World's Largest Surf Shop, covering 52,000 square feet and it complements the nearby Ron Jon Watersports Shop. If you ever have a rainy day in Cocoa Beach, this is a great place to hang out!

As well as catching the rays on the sandy beach, you can go kayaking, sport fishing, take an airboat ride, go parasailing, take surf lessons or spot Florida wildlife from an airboat ride at Midway. Cocoa Beach has a few restaurants and shops selling beachwear, shells and clothing. You may not be able to do your weekly shop there but you will find plenty of places to rent and buy beach gear and maybe even get a tattoo!

The gorgeous sandy beach is lined with hotels and holiday apartments to accommodate guests. Many more day-trippers take a day off from Orlando, 60 miles away, to enjoy a day relaxing on Cocoa Beach. Casual beach bars and restaurants overlook the beach and places like The Beach Shack and Coconuts on the Beach offer good food, live music and the occasional bikini contest.

Things to Do in Cocoa Beach

There are plenty of excellent things to do around Cocoa Beach. Take a stroll along the pier or visit Jetty Park where you can go fishing and watch cruise ships sail by from the beach. A day at the Kennedy Space Center is a must for families of all ages. See the launch pads, explore the Space Garden and get a virtual experience of a Space Shuttle launch. There are many 3D film experiences and exhibits telling the history of the Space Race.

One of the most popular activities for all ages is the two-hour boat trip with Island Boat Line Eco Tours through the small barrier islands known as Thousand Islands on the Banana River, part of the Indian River Lagoon. Tours depart from the East Merritt Island Causeway near the sunset Waterfront Grill and Bar. The trips are on pontoon boats on calm waters and are led by a certified captain and a professional naturalist. They do a great job of spotting wildlife, including herons, alligators, frogs, turtles and usually an endangered manatee or two. In the nesting season, the island trees are covered in herons, egrets and even pelicans, sitting on their huge nests.

The Luxury Resort of Palm Beach Florida

The very name "Palm Beach "conjures up the image of exclusive boutiques, high-end restaurants and millionaire mansions, but you don't have to be uber-rich to enjoy this lovely Florida resort. Palm Beach is on a long barrier island, just off the coast of southeast Florida, 70 miles north of Miami. It is the easternmost town in Florida and has a year-round population of 10,000, which triples in the winter months with snowbird visitors. This desirable town has a high number of wealthy residents, many of whom are Russian or Austrian.

History of Palm Beach

Palm Beach only came into being in the early 1900s when railroad tycoon Henry Morrison Flagler built the Florida East Coast Railway along the Florida coastline. He originally visited St Augustine for his wife's health and saw the potential of Florida as a winter haven. Having already made a fortune with his company, Standard Oil, he started a second career building a railroad all the way to Key West.

Flagler chose Palm Beach to build two luxury hotels, the Royal Poinciana and the Breakers Hotel, which is still an exclusive five star hotel today. He also built himself a stunning Beaux-Arts mansion, Whitehall, in 1902 that now offers informative guided tours.

The town of Palm Beach was incorporated in 1911 and by then was already attracting the Who's Who of New York society. Many black employees, who worked as servants in the mansions, rented small homes in an area called the Styx. The landowners agreed to evict all these tenants, who were moved to West Palm Beach, and the land was sold for development.

Things to Do in Palm Beach

The gorgeous beach is the number one attraction in Palm Beach. It offers fine white sand and clear Atlantic waters. Take a beach chair and enjoy the sound of the waves gently turning along the seashore or watch the many boats sailing by. Even the odd cruise ship can be seen heading for the nearby ports of Fort Lauderdale and Miami.

The Four Arts Gardens are botanical gardens of note, established in 1938 and now maintained by the Garden Club of Palm Beach. They were designed as a series of themed garden rooms. Look for the moongate and statues in the Chinese Garden, the decorative well, and the fountain in the Madonna Garden.

Worth Avenue is where the rich and famous come to browse and drop their dollars. Known as "The Avenue", luxury brand names such as Chanel, Gucci, Valentino, Dior and Saks Fifth Avenue line this beautiful street. The Galleria of Sculpture and the John H. Surovek Gallery are well worth browsing. City Place is a more regular place to shop, with national chain stores such as Macy's and Williams-Sonoma. A free trolley transports visitors to and from this palm-lined shopper's paradise, located across the Intracoastal Waterway on Rosemary Ave.

For eating and drinking you can choose from Starbucks, the Japanese Steakhouse or one of the local favorites such as Renato's or the Trevini Restorante, but you may want to check the prices first!

Historic Buildings in Palm Beach

The Breakers Hotel is a wonderfully located historic hotel surrounded by lush gardens. It is on the National Register of Historic Places and is strictly gated.

The Flagler Museum and tour of the Whitehall mansion make a truly enjoyable day out in Palm Beach. Whitehall was designed around an open-air courtyard with a beautiful ballroom and it still has Flagler's railroad car in the garden. Another splendid landmark mansion in Palm Beach is Mar-a-Lago, built by socialite Marjorie Merriweather Post and the location of many charitable balls. It is now privately owned by Donald Trump.

Boca Raton – a City for All Seasons

Boca Raton, pronounced "Boca Ratone", is an upmarket city 45 miles north of Miami and 28 miles south of West Palm Beach. Located on the Atlantic coast, it was the dream of architect Addison Mizner who also created West Palm Beach, hence the similarities in architecture and style. Initial advertisements for the newly developing city announced, "I am the greatest resort in the world!" However, that did not manifest itself during Mizner's lifetime.

South Beach Gazebo, Boca Raton

Boca Raton consists of high-end shopping malls, corporate HQs and country club estates with a range of luxury housing, from low-rise condos to ostentatious mansions. Most homes overlook immaculate golf courses with a tennis club onsite for added appeal. Catering mainly to middle and upper class retirees, Boca Raton has a median age of 45.4 years, according to the Sun Sentinel. Of the 84,000 inhabitants in 2011, just 3.9% were children under the age five, 3.5% were residents over the age of 85 and there were more women than men.

History of Boca Raton

Boca, as it is locally known, was incorporated in 1925, but the first settler was T.M. Rickards who lived in a house made of driftwood from 1895. Boca Raton is Spanish for "mouth of a rat" and the name appeared on 18th century maps at the closed inlet of the inland waterway known as Boca Ratones Lagoon.

In 1904, Japanese farmers at the Yamato colony planted the land with pineapples. Later, during World War II, much of this land was confiscated and used to build the Boca Raton Army Air Force base. It is now the campus of the Florida Atlanta University.

The 1920s saw a land boom across Florida as the railroad opened up the possibility for wealthy East Coast families to winter further south. Mizner developed the ultra-luxurious Ritz Carlton Cloister Inn in 1926, which later became the Boca Raton Resort and Club. It had 100 rooms and was the most expensive hotel in the U.S. at that time.

Today the hotel operates as the Waldorf Astoria Resort and private community, complete with golf course. Located beside the Intracoastal Waterway, it is often referred to as the "pink hotel" and has retained much of its original Spanish style with classical water features, serene pools and a bar overlooking the beach and ocean. It is well worth dining there for the location and historic experience.

The plan to create a masterpiece of city planning from this pineapple-growing area was curtailed when Florida's real estate bubble burst in 1926. After World War II, Mizner's plans were resurrected and today Boca Raton is one of Florida's most affluent cities.

Highlights of Boca Raton

The Town Hall on Palmetto Park Road has some interesting exhibits relating to Boca's short history. You can book a tour of the original Boca Raton Resort and Club from the Town Hall which is conducted by the Boca Raton Historical Society.

Just across the road from the Town Hall is the impressive Mizner Park, one of several dazzling malls serving the community. Beautifully designed, it typifies the city's status. Even more chi-chi is the Royal Palm Plaza with designer boutiques arranged around Spanish-style courtyards, but it is very pleasant to wander around and window-shop.

Of most historical interest is the Old Floresta district, about one mile west of the Town Hall. This is a collection of 29 Mediterranean style homes that Mizner designed and built for his company directors and is a worthwhile place to explore.

Things to Do Around Boca Raton

Visitors to the Boca area will find plenty to see and do. Fabulous shopping, dozens of restaurants to suit all budgets and tastes, and several interesting attractions are all designed to fill the days when thousands of snowbirds come to town, from November to April.

Museums and Art Galleries

The Boca Raton Museum of Art has a tasteful collection of 19th and 20th century artworks including charcoal drawings by Picasso and Matisse. Located on W. Palmetto Park Road, this compact gallery houses the Mayers Collection.

More lighthearted is the International Museum of Cartoon Art featuring 160,000 cartoons ranging from Peanuts to politics. The collection was created in 1974 and was moved to its modern purpose-built home within Mizner Park in 1996. The collection has cartoons from all over the world dating back to the 19th century. The attraction includes a theater and a Laughter Center to show how laughter is good for your health!

The Sports Immortals Museum on N. Federal Highway has 10,000 mementoes of sporting history. Baseball fans can drool over Babe Ruth's baseball bat alongside Mohammed Ali's boxing robes. The most valuable piece is perhaps the most insignificant. It is a rare cigarette card featuring a baseball player who objected to his image being associated with tobacco. It was quickly withdrawn, hence the value of the surviving card - $600,000!

Gardens, Parks and Beaches

Further north, the Morikami Museum and Japanese Gardens is a truly tranquil and colorful area designed around a lake overlooked by a traditional Japanese teahouse. The gardens are a tribute to the Yamato Colony of Japanese who were the first real farmers in the Boca area.

Boca Raton's beach is a long unspoiled stretch of dunes with soft white sand that this coast is famous for. Located north of the Boca Raton inlet, the beach is accessed from Ocean Boulevard through various parks such as the Spanish River Park, which has picnic tables and a wildlife observation tower overlooking the Intracoastal Waterway.

The Red Reef Park Beach further south offers boardwalks over the dunes and an artificial offshore reef for snorkeling. Right next door is the Gumbo Limbo Nature Center, which has an excellent educational center and overlooks Lake Wyman, part of the Intracoastal Waterway.

Boca is one of those places you either love or loathe. Almost too good to be true, it nonetheless offers an enviable lifestyle with glorious sunshine, great shopping and beautiful beaches.

Fort Lauderdale – Yachting Capital of the World

Fort Lauderdale is a pleasant high-rise resort city with high-end shopping malls, a pleasant Riverwalk lined with mega-yachts and a beautiful palm-fringed white sandy beach. Although relatively compact, it has everything that visitors are looking for in a winter sun destination.

The city of Fort Lauderdale has grown from a busy trading post on the New River in the 1900s to the modern metropolis it is today, thanks to its many waterways. This was what first led to the three forts being built here during the Seminole Wars and has since allowed it to develop as one of the busiest cruise ports in the world.

Las Olas Boulevard

Most visitors head for Las Olas Boulevard which is lined with interesting shops, boutiques and galleries. In the evenings, tables spill out across the sidewalk and make the most of the pleasant temperatures and vibrant atmosphere after dark. Formal eateries blend with casual dining and there is always a long line waiting for a table at the popular Cheesecake Factory. More upmarket is the swish Jackson's Steakhouse with its private club ambience.

Fort Lauderdale Riverwalk

Leading off from Las Olas Boulevard is the 1½-mile long Riverwalk, a meandering landscaped pathway along the north bank of the New River. It passes towering glass high-rise buildings, luxury sea-going yachts and eventually reaches the modern shopping district. There are several waterfront pubs offering tasty lunches, evening meals or sunset cocktails at Happy Hour overlooking the river. Enjoy people-watching and see the bridge lift from time to time to let tall-masted yachts sail up-river.

Further along the waterfront is Stranrahan House, the oldest surviving building in the city. It was once the site of the city's first trading post, post office and bank. It is now restored to its heyday of 1901 with typical Floridian furnishings and old photographs of Frank Stranrahan trading alligator hides, otter skins and egret feathers with the native Seminoles. It's hard to think how much this area has changed in just a century!

Continue along through the park-like area to the Broward Center for the Performing Arts which always has a varied program in its two theaters.

Boat Trips

From the waterfront, visitors can take a one or two-hour cruise of the waterways on a modern cruise boat. Nearby the old Jungle Queen paddle-wheeler offers onboard shows and barbecue buffets. Cruises sail around The Isles, a series of man-made canals dug in the 1920s. Multi-million-dollar mansions look out across swimming pools to luxury yachts moored at the end of the garden.

The waterways eventually lead out to Port Everglades which has many container ships and oil tankers. The separate cruise port area is perpetually busy with huge cruise ships coming and going to the Bahamas, the Caribbean and further afield.

Things to Do in Old Fort Lauderdale

Second Avenue is where most of the historical houses in Fort Lauderdale can be found. These plantation-style homes have shady verandas and sit amid lush tropical gardens. Many of the buildings are administered by the Fort Lauderdale Historical Society from their base at the Historical Museum.

Highlights to look out for are the King-Cromartie House, built on the south bank of the river in 1907 and transported by barge to its present position in 1971 to preserve it.

Behind the house is Fort Lauderdale's first schoolhouse, built in 1899. The old brick buildings around Southwest 2nd Street are a great place to find a tempting lunch or iced coffee.

Bonnet House in a plantation-style historic home overlooking the Intracoastal Waterway. Guided tours of this furnished home and gardens will reveal a wonderful collection of post-impressionist artworks, a dining room with real turtle shells decorating the walls, a circular Shell Room and a splendid Orchid House full of blooms.

Bonnet House - courtesy David Warren

Also in this area is the Museum of Science and Discovery which is deservedly popular. It shows Florida wildlife in recreated ecoscapes and a range of realistic films in the IMAX Theater. The neighbouring Museum of Art is in an impressive post-modernist building and showcases CoBrA artworks. These are works by expressionist painters from Copenhagen, Brussels and Amsterdam, hence the strange acronym.

From here, a hop-on, hop-off trolley tour links this downtown area with the beach which is truly beautiful. A narrow strip of white sand runs beside the bluest Atlantic waves. The paved promenade is shaded by many palm trees giving the area a truly tropical appeal and is enjoyed by walkers, cyclists and roller-bladers

Miami and Miami Beach

Miami is at the southernmost tip of Florida and is like nowhere else in the world. This cosmopolitan city is the home of the American Airlines Arena (base for the Miami Heat Basketball Team), the Performing Arts Centre and the regenerated area along the banks of the Miami River.

Miami is totally tropical in its climate and in its vibrant culture. Temperatures throughout the year range from 75-90°F (23-32°C) during the day with heavy afternoon showers from July to November, along with the occasional threat of a hurricane. The warm sunny winters attract many snowbirds and wealthy families to enjoy their winter homes in the city. Once known for its gangland violence and total disregard for prohibition in the 1920s, it is now a chic playground for the rich and famous. The city of Miami is an eclectic mix of ultra-modern high-rise condos, modern shopping malls, upmarket beach resorts and poorer neighborhoods.

Miami Beach is on the outlying barrier island to the east of the city of Miami. It is linked to the mainland by several causeways including the MacArthur Causeway, the Venetian Causeway, and just a little further north by the Julia Tuttle Causeway. The waterway between the city of Miami and Miami Beach is known as Biscayne Bay, part of the Intracoastal Waterway that runs all the way up the eastern seaboard to New York.

Within Biscayne Bay there are several manmade islands which are private, occupied by some of Miami's most desirable multi-million dollar properties with luxury yachts moored alongside. Hibiscus Island, Palm Island and Star Island are just some of these manmade islands – easily defined from the air by their very geometric shapes!

Miami is a major center for finance, commerce, entertainment, media, sport and the arts. It is known as the "Gateway to the Americas" and has a large Hispanic population from Cuba, Colombia and South America. In fact over half the population of Miami speaks Spanish as their first language! The plus side is that you can get great international cuisine in the city, from authentic Cuban sandwiches to great Brazilian churrascarias.

Miami Districts

The city of Miami has around 400,000 residents although the metro area actually has over 5.5 million residents. Miami is divided into a number of districts. Brickell is the most affluent area with modern high-rise architecture that is home to international bank headquarters, lawyers' offices and some of Miami's most exclusive luxury hotels and condos.

To the south of the city is Coral Gables, known for its huge old fig trees and mansions. The historic Biltmore Hotel and Golf Course are in this area and have been entertaining presidents, celebrities and royalty since the hotel opened in 1926. Some of Miami's best shopping can be found along Bird Road and in the Merrick Park Mall in Coral Gables.

West of Downtown Miami is the airport, surrounded by districts that tell their own story – Little Havana, Hialeah, Upper East Side, Opa-Locka and Miami Shores. Further north lie Miami Gardens, Golden Glades and North Miami Beach, not to be confused with Miami Beach, which is across the causeway.

Miami Beach is known for its gorgeous white sands and azure blue waters. The boardwalk is the place for beautiful people to stroll and be seen. Miami Beach also has its own famous neighborhoods including the Art Deco hotels and restaurants along Ocean Drive in South Beach, or SoBe as it likes to be known.

South Pointe is at the very tip of South Beach and overlooks the entrance to one of the busiest cruise ports in the world. Huge cruise ships glide in and out, regularly heading for the Caribbean or the Bahamas. Further north is Miami Beach itself with the Lincoln Road Mall, Jackie Gleason Theater and the Miami Beach Convention Center. North Beach leads on to Surfside and snobbish Bal Harbour, with its exclusive designer shopping mall.

Further west from Miami the road quickly hits the Everglades National Park, one of the natural wonders of the world, but that's a story for another day!

South Beach from South Pointe

Key Biscayne - Bill Baggs Cape Florida State Park

If you fancy visiting one of the Top 10 Beaches in North America, at least according to "Dr. Beach", aka Stephen Leatherman, then head down to Key Biscayne, just south of downtown Miami. Accessed via the Rickenbacker Causeway (small toll payable), you find yourself a castaway on a tropical island beach just minutes after leaving the choking traffic of Brickell Ave, Miami.

Cape Florida Lighthouse

Drive past Crandon Park Golf Course on the right and look for parking beside the three-mile-long stretch of sand and shallow warm waters in Crandon Park. Walk the boardwalk, sit beneath the palm trees, pick up a cold drink or sit and watch families having fun on the sand and in the sea.

If you drive on further, you will pass some desirable condos on the left hand side along with the plush Ritz Carlton Resort and several beach shops, mini-malls and restaurants.

Keep on until you enter the green oasis of Bill Baggs Cape Florida State Park. If you drive right to the far end of Crandon Blvd, you come to the Cape Florida Lighthouse.

Things to Do on Key Biscayne

Built in 1825, Cape Florida Lighthouse was reconstructed in 1846, after being damaged during the Second Seminole War. This historic black and white lighthouse is the oldest standing structure in Miami-Dade County - even South Beach was not built until the early 20th century.

Guided tours of the lighthouse and the nearby lighthouse-keeper's cottage are available twice daily, Thursdays through Mondays at 10am and 1pm. There is a video presentation and 109 spiral steps to climb if you want to enjoy the view. Beneath the lighthouse there are a couple of eateries – the Lighthouse Café and the Boater's Grill which offer mainly Cuban cuisine and meat-packed deli sandwiches.

If you have brought your own picnic, make use of the picnic tables or reserve the pavilion and light up the grill. Beach chairs, bicycles and umbrellas can all be rented to make the most of a day at this "Top 10" beach. It offers a mile of postcard-pretty white sand, washed by the Atlantic that just begs you to dive in and cool off.

Brief History of Key Biscayne

It was Ponce de Leon who named this area "Cape Florida" when he led the first Spanish expedition of discovery in 1513. The island was once a secret meeting place and port for runaway slaves and black Seminoles who sought passage to the Bahamas offshore. Sea captains no doubt made a good living from this human smuggling trade until the Cape Florida Lighthouse was built, bringing their dubious activities to a swift end!

The original state park was simply named Cape Florida State Park, but in 1971 it was renamed in honor of Bill Baggs, the Editor of the Miami News. He was influential in bringing about the purchase of the land and securing the beauty of Key Biscayne for future generations to enjoy .In 1992 Key Biscayne suffered massive damage from the 160 m.p.h. winds of Hurricane Andrew. Restrooms, concession stands and even trees were flattened.

Today it is a piece of paradise with good amenities yet it retains its natural beauty and is a wonderful place to walk, bicycle, swim and sunbathe against the backdrop of Miami's high-rises in one direction and blue seas in the other.

Key West – America's Southernmost City

The isolated island of Key West marks the southernmost point of the United States. Situated at the end of the 106-mile long Overseas Highway that links the chain of islands at the southern tip of Florida, Key West has inevitably developed as a haven for artists, writers, divers, fishing enthusiasts and those wanting to escape run-of-the-mill life in mainstream America.

Getting to Key West

Until the Florida East Coast Railway was built from Miami to Key West in 1912, this tiny community was accessible only by boat. Visitors today arrive by private boat, car, airplane into the tiny airport, ferry from Fort Myers, or by cruise ship. The railway line never recovered from devastating damage caused by the category five hurricane on Labor Day in 1935 when a storm surge of 18-20 feet damaged not only the railway but also many of the upper Florida Keys. The surviving infrastructure of the railway was used as a foundation for extending the two-lane US-1 from Miami to Key West, completed in 1938.

Things to Do in Key West

Key West covers a total area of just 7.4 square miles and its high point is a mere 18 feet above sea level. What it lacks in size it makes up for in spirit, with a lively celebration at sunset each evening on Mallory Square. Locals and visitors alike gather to toast the sun going down and to look for the green flash that can occasionally be seen as the sun's orb disappears below the horizon. Cocktails are served from surrounding bars and street entertainers are on hand to offer some amazing performances at this nightly party. Jugglers, magicians, buskers and animal trainers all mix with tattooed bikers and yuppie yacht-owners at this vibrant sunset celebration.

After dark the action moves to Duval Street, where bars host live bands and wet T-shirt contests. One of the best known locations is Sloppy Joe's, once the haunt of writer Ernest Hemingway. Alternatively, join the fun at Jimmy Buffet's Margaritaville Café nearby.

Hemingway's House

The buildings and mansions in the Key West Historic District (including Mallory Square and Duval Street) were mostly built between 1886 and 1912. The charming Victorian architecture contains some of Key West's museums and is painted in charming pastel colors now known as "Key West style". The New Town was developed on a landfill site in the 1940s and includes the airport, schools, motels, residential areas and shopping malls.

One of Key West's most famous residents was President Harry Truman who once resided in the Little White House. This delightful building now houses a museum of his life. Ernest Hemingway wrote several of his well-known novels during his time at 907 Whitehead Street, in a house given to him and his wife Pauline as a wedding present in 1931. The house is now a popular museum of his life and works and is still populated by the many-toed cats that Hemingway kept as pets.

Southernmost House

There are a host of activities in Key West to suit every age and taste. Stroll the streets picking up souvenirs or browse the many colorful art galleries. Take a tour on the Conch Train that runs around the island's landmarks offering an informative commentary or visit the mansions and gardens which depict the tropical Key West lifestyle. Enjoy a snorkeling or diving trip in these clear waters or join a sport fishing charter for some of the most exciting fishing around. Visit the old lighthouse or spend the day relaxing on the soft white sand of Smathers Beach where the shallow waters are always warm.

Naples - Florida's Golf Capital

Like many cities in southern Florida, Naples was first born on paper by far-sighted land speculators back in the 1880s. The area, situated on the Gulf Coast about 115 miles due west of Ft Lauderdale, had been promoted by many magazines and newspapers praising the mild winter climate and excellent fishing. When investors described its beauty as "surpassing the bay in Naples, Italy", the name stuck and Naples, Florida was put on the map.

Naples Zoo

In 1887, a group of developers led by Walter N. Haldeman, publisher of the Louisville Courier-Journal, and his partner Kentucky Senator John Stuart Williams, bought up 8,700 acres of beachfront. They had plans drawn up for a town and sold off the land in lots,

Downtown Naples

The downtown area of Old Naples is a delightful place to visit and stroll around. Buildings, many of which date back to the early 20th century, remain mercifully low-level and lush tropical vegetation makes it a very pleasant place to explore. Sidewalks cafés and restaurants, art galleries, boutiques brimming with Caribbean cruise wear and upmarket gift shops line the main shopping street on Fifth Avenue. Slightly set back from the promenading shoppers is Blackburn Hall, home to the Naples Players who provide an entertaining program of music and drama throughout the year.

From the town center, avenues decorated with gnarled Poinciana trees, banyans and king palms radiate out, lined with pastel-colored mansions and plantation-style winter homes. The city reflects its cosmopolitan heritage with Irish pubs, Italian pizzerias, Thai restaurants, a New England Seafood Chowder House and even the Jolly Cricket with its Brit-themed menu.

Naples Beach

Follow Fifth Avenue South to the extreme end and you will arrive at one of the most idyllic beaches in Florida. The narrow strip of white powder-soft sand is lined with leaning palm trees. The glittering Gulf waters toss tiny shells ashore in the gentle white-foamed waves and you can understand why visitors vow that this is where they dream of retiring to. And many of them do.

Further south, at the terminus of 12th Ave, Naples pier protrudes into the blue waters and is a popular resting place for both anglers and pelicans. The original pier was built in 1887 and stretched for 600 feet. It was destroyed by Hurricane Donna in 1960, along with many of the original 19th century homes. Also on 12th Ave is Palm Cottage, the winter home of founder Walter Haldeman, built in 1895 and now a local museum.

Things to Do in Naples Florida

The combination of sunshine and retirees inevitably spells golf and it is said there are more golf holes per capita in Naples than anywhere else in Florida. Currently there are more than 80 championship golf courses providing pleasant green space within most of the outlying retirement communities. The population of Naples is over 21,000, with both the average age and median income being higher than most other Florida cities.

Naples Botanical Gardens

Along with nearby Marco Island and the Everglades National Park, Naples' economy is largely based upon tourism. As well as its beautiful shell-strewn beaches, Naples has several other attractions including Naples Botanical gardens, Naples Zoo at Caribbean Gardens, Corkscrew Swamp Sanctuary, Big Cypress National Preserve and the Florida Panther National Wildlife Refuge, making it a great place to visit for all ages.

Corkscrew Swamp Sanctuary

Fort Myers and Sanibel Island

Fort Myers, known as the City of Palms, is a thriving city and the seat of Lee County. Barely more than 120 years old, this city has an interesting history as it developed from a waterside swamp to become the Gateway to Southwest Florida. With a beautiful winter climate and riverfront position, it was the chosen place for Thomas Edison and Henry Ford to build their winter homes. These adjoining properties are now a major local attraction.

First Street, Fort Myers

Early Seminole Indian History in Fort Myers

The indigenous Seminole Indians of Florida were driven further south with each new treaty. When cattlemen wanted their final territory for grazing their cattle, Congress offered the Seminoles a bounty to move west, but this was one move too much, so they refused. This led to tensions and in early 1850 a military fort was reactivated on the Caloosahatchee River as a base of operations. It was previously known as Fort Harvie but was re-named after Colonel Abraham Myers, and so Fort Myers was born, at least in name.

This waterfront fort was a sizeable compound with 57 buildings, a hospital and gardens. It was kept supplied by Manuel Gonzales, in his sloop. After eight years of strife, Indian Chief Billy Bowlegs and his warriors surrendered and the fort was finally abandoned. Billy Creek, which flows into the Caloosahatchee River near Dean Park, was named after the camp where Billy Bowlegs and his followers waited for ships to transport them west.

Civil War Battle of Fort Myers

In 1863, the fort was occupied by Union Army troops during the Civil War. In early 1865, three companies of Florida militia attacked the fort, tired of the cattle raids launched against the local ranches. After sporadic fighting, the Confederates retreated, in what became known as the Battle of Fort Myers. However, just a month later the Union troops abandoned Fort Myers altogether.

Early Settlement of Fort Myers

First settlers arrived in the Fort Myers area around 1866. Manuel Gonzales, the former supplier to the fort, returned and repaired a house to live in, and then moved there with his family. They operated a trading post where the present Federal building now stands. Mrs. Gonzales became the first schoolteacher for the community that developed around it.

The city of Fort Myers was officially established in 1886. It became known as a desirable winter resort when the Royal Palm Hotel opened in 1898. Around this time Tootie McGregor, along with Thomas and Mina Edison, began beautifying Fort Myers. They donated royal palms to be planted along Riverside Drive which was renamed McGregor Blvd. in Tootie's honor. These graceful palms are now 75 feet tall and provide an impressive guard of honor to all who arrive in Fort Myers today.

In 1902, Manuel Gonzales was obviously settled and prospering. He built two houses on the corner of Broadway and Second Street, in the heart of present-day Fort Myers. He moved his family into one house and his mother lived in the other.

In 1904, the railway arrived in Fort Myers, further developing the community along with the building of the Tamiami Trail (now US 41) across the Caloosahatchee River in 1924.

Much later, in the 1970s, the two Gonzales houses were amalgamated by Peter Pulitzer, son of the well-known publisher. He created a home for his fishing buddy, Fingers O'Bannon. In 1978, the buildings were bought by Paul Peden who transformed them into the Veranda, a well-known upscale restaurant with a splendid reputation for good food. These restored turn-of-the-century homes have an authentic atmosphere and make this a charming place to have lunch or dinner in the heart of downtown Fort Myers.

Fort Myers Beach

Fort Myers Beach lies almost 15 miles south of downtown Fort Myers. It runs along the barrier islands of Estero and San Carlos for about six miles before merging into Lovers Key State Park. The town of Fort Myers Beach has around 6,000 residents. The beachfront is lined with beach homes of all ages and sizes, along with some small vacation condo buildings, several churches, shopping plazas and motels.

Once the San Carlos Blvd reaches the beach it turns sharp left and runs parallel to the beach along Estero Blvd. At this corner Times Square offers parking and there is a playground for children, volleyball courts, cafés, ice cream parlors and beach shops nearby. The road in this direction eventually ends at Bowditch Pointe Recreational Park which has picnic tables, a fishing pier and is a great place to watch the sunset.

Beach parking at Fort Myers Beach is available in a number of car parks with metered spaces, or in private car parks where daily charges range upwards from $6. Close to the pier are the main attractions clustered around the Lani Kai Island Resort which has restrooms, beachfront cafés and a rooftop restaurant. In the season there are rows of umbrellas and chair rentals along with jet skis, banana boat rides and parasailing watersports. The Gulf waters are shallow, calm and warm, making it ideal for families to enjoy a day on the beach.

Further east the beach becomes increasingly less commercialized and crowded. Boats can be hired from the Matanzas Pass Preserve for exploring the quiet calm waterways that are strewn with small islands.

Sanibel Island

If you visit Fort Myers, you are within striking distance of the destination that travel author, Arthur Frommer, ranked as his favorite place. He listed Sanibel Island, a barrier island just off Fort Myers, above even Bali and Paris. Although the island says this prestige gives them a sense of security, with the attention of the world headed in its direction, perhaps Sanibel and neighboring Captiva will not remain peaceful for long.

Fortunately the island has long had a strict building code, enabling both these tropical islands to remain unspoiled hidden treasures. Sanibel's tropical natural beauty includes long shell-covered beaches with palm trees leaning lazily overhead providing welcome shade. The Gulf waters are clear, shallow and warm, making paddling a pleasure. The island is also home to many rare birds, particularly in the migrating season, thanks to the protected reserves within the Ding Darling National Wildlife Refuge.

Sanibel Island is reached via a new bridge, completed in 2007, and there is a toll to get onto the island. There is also a further charge if you wish to visit the Wildlife Reserve, so it is not a cheap place to check out. However, if you plan to bring a picnic and make a day of it, there is plenty to see and do for your money.

Things to Do on Sanibel Island

The island is best known for its shells that wash up ankle deep along the gentle waterline of this Gulf Coast paradise. The removal of live shells is strictly permitted, so check each "dwelling" before you pop it in your bag. These beaches offer some of the best shelling in the world, from magnificent conch to tiny pink pearl shells, and everything in between. Visitors walk along the shore bent over, addicted to spotting the next shell…and the next. It is such a common sight that visitors are said to be performing the "Sanibel Stoop"!

If you want to see some of the best shell specimens, visit the Bailey-Matthews Shell Museum where you can learn how to recognize some of the shells and learn about their former inhabitants. Admission is currently $9 for adults and includes access to the many exhibits. The Great Hall of Shells has displays of shells in family groups and claims to have one third of the 10,000 species found all over the world.

The J.N.Ding Darling National Wildlife Refuge covers 5,200 acres of Sanibel Island to protect the mangroves and the dependent wildlife and birds. Broad trails run for 5 miles through the reserve and visitors can explore on foot, bicycle, tram, car or kayak to see alligators, anhingas, great egrets, snowy egrets, ospreys, roseate spoonbills, bald eagles, wood storks, tri-colored herons, greater and little blue herons. The refuge was formed in memory of cartoonist J.N.Ding Darling by his family and friends. It is run by many volunteers along with a team of professional staff.

Venice - Shark's Tooth Capital of the World

Venice is a mid-sized city on the coast of Sarasota County, just south of Tampa Bay. This vacation hotspot is well-known for its miles of soft white sands that offer safe swimming, sunbathing, boating, surfing and shell collecting opportunities.

Often described as an old railroad town, Venice mixes its history with a more modern and progressive side, as a popular vacation resort. The well-preserved buildings and architectural heritage of downtown Venice from the 1900s add a touch of character to this modern city. Venice has several buildings on the National Register of Historic Places including the Hotel Venice, Triangle Inn, Blalock House, the Venice Depot, Levillain-Letton House and the Edgewood and Eagle Point Historic Districts.

Venice Early History

One of the first settlers to the area was Richard Roberts in the 1870s and he built a home near what became known as Roberts Bay. In 1884, Frank Higel moved to the area and he began a citrus business. His family diversified into boat building, fishing and contracting. When Darwin Curry was appointed the first postmaster, Curry and Higel agreed upon the name of Venice for the community, and so it has remained.

With the arrival of the railroad in 1911, the town began to develop. City planner John Nolan laid out the original city plan in 1926 along with the Brotherhood of Locomotive Engineers (BLE) Corporation. The town council, police and fire departments followed shortly after and Edward Worthington was made the first mayor in 1927. The town expanded further with the establishing of the Venice Army Air Base in 1942.

Not all of Venice's fame has been positive. In 2001, Robert Hanssen was charged with spying for the KGB and Venice hit the newspapers, as his mother lived in the city. Later that year it was also discovered that three of the hijackers responsible for the September 11 attacks had all lived in Venice for a time and had trained at a private flight school at Venice Municipal Airport. Despite its notoriety, Venice remains a popular place for family vacations and snowbirds.

Things to Do in Venice

Known for their safe swimming and water sports, the beaches of Venice do have something rather unique. They are known as the "Shark's Tooth Capital of the World". Take a walk along Caspersen Beach and keep a sharp lookout for the triangular shaped fossilized teeth which have a distinctive curve and can be anything up to three inches long. You will see many serious sharks' tooth hunters sifting the sand with their special wire baskets, looking for these interesting collectibles.

Shark's tooth – ½ in

Another unusual beach attraction is the drum circle that gathers every Saturday at sunset on Nokomis Beach. The drummers beat out the sun, accompanied by energetic dancers. I guess even the Native Indians would have approved of this local tradition!

Stylish St Petersburg and St Pete Beach

What draws thousands of visitors every year to St Petersburg, Florida? The sunny climate, 28 miles of barrier island beaches, watersports and a host of cultural attractions is probably the answer.

Photo Dali Museum courtesy of Visit Tampa Bay

Situated on a peninsula overlooking Tampa Bay and midway down the Gulf Coast of Florida, this buzzing community has around 245,000 residents – and thousands more visitors just passing through.

The city is more often referred to as St Pete, a nod to its satellite beach on the outlying barrier islands called St Pete Beach. This popular resort officially changed its name in 1994 to sound more hip and it lies 10 miles east of the city of St Petersburg.

At one time the city of St Petersburg had a reputation as "God's waiting room" as it was popular with ageing snowbirds and retirees. However, international visitors and young families have awakened this city to its true potential and it now enjoys a much more vibrant atmosphere.

St Petersburg boasts 360 days of sunshine a year and has certainly earned the nickname "The Sunshine City". It was developed, like much of Florida, in the 19th century.

Michigan farmer, John Williams, saw the potential for Florida's coast and bought an area of land on Tampa Bay in 1875 with dreams of building a huge city. Russian nobleman, Peter Demens, provided the area with a railroad and the city was named after his birthplace – St Petersburg in Russia.

Alas, St Petersburg, Florida lacks the stunning architecture, onion-domed palaces and breathtaking cathedral of its Imperial Baltic namesake, but it does have some pretty unique architecture. The eye-catching pier with its inverted triangular building is the main landmark of the city. This upside-down pyramid houses shops, restaurants, an observation deck and an aquarium, so it is a neat place to visit.

Things to Do in St Petersburg, Florida

From the pier, a trolley bus runs along the seafront to the Great Explorations attraction, an arts and science museum mainly geared towards children. It includes some physical challenges such as a climbing wall and a Touch Tunnel where you clamber through a 90-foot-long tunnel in the dark, touching various sensory exhibits.

If you are into modern art and appreciate the acclaimed works of Salvador Dali, the museum in his name has the most comprehensive collection of his works in the world. This $350 million collection was amassed by Reynolds Morse and his partner, Eleanor. They became lifelong friends with Dali after buying one of his paintings. They chose to put the collection on display in St Petersburg as they felt it most closely resembled the artist's home town of Cadaques in Spain.

Another place to visit in this city of broad avenues is the Sunken Gardens on 4th St N. It has extensive orchids, water features and aviaries amidst exotic tropical plants. It certainly makes a pleasant retreat from the busy city.

Just south of the city is Fort de Soto Park, which has great views of the Sunshine Skyway Bridge, a magnificent feat of engineering crossing Tampa Bay. The park has some beautiful beaches, bird colonies and the remains of the Fort de Soto, begun during the Spanish-American War in 1898.

Tampa – Cigar City

Tampa is the largest city on the Gulf Coast of Florida. It is situated on the north side of the huge Tampa Bay with Bradenton to the south and St Petersburg to the west.

Although Spanish explorers visited the Tampa Bay area in 1528, there was no permanent settlement for another 300 years. In 1824 the U.S. government created a reservation for the Seminole Indians and manned Fort Brooke to protect both the reservation and the natural harbor. Things were slow to progress until 1883 when phosphate was discovered, which in turn led to the railroad being built from Tampa to Jacksonville by Henry B. Plant.

Not content with his railroad achievements, Plant went on to develop the Grand Plant Hotel, promoting Tampa as a warm winter resort destination and eventually the idea took hold with wealthy Americans from the northern states.

Ybor City

One of the most unique areas to the east of Tampa is historic Ybor City, often considered part of downtown. This historic cigar-making area has a strong Cuban influence, great architecture, live music and of course Cuban cuisine!

The cigar-making business began in 1886 when Vincente Ybor opened his first cigar factory in Ybor City. Spanish, Cuban and Sicilian workers flocked to the area for work.

By the turn of the century the Spanish American War had broken out and Tampa then became the main point for deploying troops to Cuba. Cigar production reached its peak in 1929, when the factories turned out 500,000,000 cigars; coincidentally this was the year that the Great Depression began.

The best way to learn about the history of the area is by visiting the Ybor City State Museum to see the unique exhibits. Fascinating walking tours of Ybor City take place every Saturday at 10.30am and longer tours can be arranged midweek. There is an Art Walk on the first Saturday in the month with great arts and crafts on display, and on the last Saturday in the month as part of "Guavaveeb" there is a night time parade.

West Tampa

Another clearly defined area is West Tampa, a residential area stretching from the Raymond James Stadium and Tampa International Airport up to Pinellas County.

Modern-day Tampa

During the 20th century, Tampa became a flourishing and diverse state, particularly since World War II. Nowadays the 335,000 population swells during the winter with the arrival of snowbirds – the non-flying variety, otherwise known as retirees! Tampa also has five cruise lines with winter cruises sailing regularly to the Caribbean and Mexico.

Things to do in Tampa

Tourists find it easy to get around this widespread city using streetcars that run from Ybor City to Dick Greco Plaza. The Florida Aquarium is a popular attraction on Channelside with touch tanks, eco-tours and interactive diving experiences.

The Tampa Museum of Art at Gasparilla Plaza is on the Hillsborough River and offers free admission on Fridays from 4-8pm. The Tampa Theater is a former movie theater and is listed on the National Register of Historic Places. It continues to have a varied program.

Busch Gardens is one of the best known attractions in Tampa with rides, shows and animal attractions. To get a good look at Florida wildlife, visit the Lowry Park Zoo which is home to everything from lorikeets to Komodo dragons and manatees. Alternatively, take a walk through Lettuce Lake Park with boardwalks around the 700-year old cypress trees that shelter birds, alligators and herons.

Tampa is sports-crazy with the Buccaneers playing football, Tampa Bay Lightning playing hockey, the Bay Rays playing baseball and several other minor leagues. Golf, shopping, excellent dining and nightlife are also plentiful in this vibrant city

Busch Gardens – "Montu" Roller Coaster

Tarpon Springs – Sponge Capital

Did you ever imagine you would find a little corner of Greece transplanted to Florida? Tarpon Springs, about 30 miles northwest of Tampa, is a historic Greek seaside community from the lovely Greek Orthodox Cathedral right down to the baklava bakeries.

Stroll down Dodecanese Street in this delightful fishing port community and you could almost believe you were in the Mediterranean. Many of the shops are owned by descendants of the first immigrants and they retain a very Greek atmosphere. Stop by one of the bakeries to pick up sticky pastries and admire the strings of natural sponges hanging outside the quaint shops.

History of Sponge Diving in Tarpon Springs

Sponge diving was the industry that attracted the first immigrants in the 19th century from the Dodecanese Islands. Natural sponges grew in abundance around the shores of the Gulf of Mexico. The Greeks had been diving for sponges around the Greek islands for centuries and they brought their skills and technical apparatus, such as it was, to Key West, and later to Tarpon Springs. At first sponges were harvested around Tarpon Springs using "hooker boats" around 1895, but by 1905 the sponges required divers to reach them. Diving for sponges was a hazardous operation. Divers wore suits weighing over 170 pounds and the heavy copper helmet had a hose for breathing. By the early 20th century over 1550 divers lived and worked in Tarpon Springs and they in turn spawned other businesses – boatyards, diving equipment suppliers, deckhands and staff to wash and sort the sponges before they were exported.

Tarpon Springs remained the "Sponge Capital of the USA" until 1946 when two disasters hit simultaneously. A red toxic tide bloomed which devastated most of the natural sponge beds and at the same time synthetic sponges were introduced to the market. Almost overnight, the sponge industry in Tarpon Springs died. The Greeks community turned their hand to fishing and tourism and that is what supports this delightful community today, along with a few sponge divers who demonstrate their skills to visitors.

The sponge warehouses have been converted into shops and the Victorian mansions now house restaurants, museums and B&Bs. It remains a Greek-American community however, with the largest concentration of Greek-Americans in the U.S.

Things to Do in Tarpon Springs

A day trip to Tarpon Springs is a real pleasure. Walk along the waterfront beside the colorful fishing fleet and tour boats near the Historic Sponge Exchange. Visit the free Spongorama Museum to see some of the antiquated equipment that is preserved here. Take a trip on a sponge-diving boat and see modern-day sponge divers at work or visit the Coral Sea Aquarium to see a living reef complete with sponges, corals and fish. Finally, enjoy an authentic Greek meal at one of the restaurants overlooking the quay.

If you are lucky there may be a traditional Greek wedding taking place at the St Nicholas Greek Orthodox Church. It was built in 1941 as a replica of St Sophia Church in Istanbul, which is said to be one of the most beautiful churches in the world. Admire the Byzantine architecture, fine religious artworks and 60 tons of Greek marble within.

Feast of Epiphany at Tarpon Springs

If you visit after Christmas, during the Feast of Epiphany on January 6 you can join in the oldest Greek Orthodox Festival outside Athens. Watch the teenage boys dive for the Epiphany Cross, tossed into the bay by the Archbishop of America. The winner receives a special blessing, not to mention boasting rights for the forthcoming year.

Cedar Key - Stilt Huts and Fishing Boats

Cedar Key is an outlying cluster of islands at the end of Hwy 24, just off US19/98 in Levy County, north central Florida. It is reached along a causeway that links the islands with the mainland. As its name suggests, Cedar Key was named after the forests of Eastern Red Cedar trees that once grew abundantly in this area.

Cedar Key Wharf

This quiet Victorian fishing village makes a great day out for visitors, offering a scenic drive along the coast before reaching the rather dilapidated buildings arranged over a few short blocks. Cedar Key's population is still under 1000.

History of Cedar Key

Early 1542 maps show Cedar Key as "Las Islas Sabines". The islands were originally inhabited by Seminole Indians and an archaeological dig at Shell Mound, 14 km north of Cedar Key, uncovered artefacts dating back to 500BC at the top of the 28-foot high mound. A 2,000 year-old skeleton was also recovered from Cedar Key in 1999, and arrowheads and spear tips from the area are said to be 12,000 years old, so it is safe to assume the islands have a long history of habitation.

Cedar Key was a known watering hole for Spanish ships and famous pirates such as Captain Kidd and Jean Lafitte in the 17th and 18th centuries. The first permanent settlement was in 1839 during the Second Seminole War, when the U.S. Army built a fort and hospital on Depot Key, later renamed Atsena Otie Key. A hurricane in 1842 caused serious damage to the fort and the Seminole Indians left the area, never to return, so Depot Key was quickly abandoned by the Army.

Gradually Florida settlers moved to the area and a post office was established in 1845. Shortly after, the lumber industry began harvesting the cedars for pencils, and cedar slats were shipped from the new port to factories further north. With the growth of the port, the Cedar Key Lighthouse was built in 1854. It stood on a 47 foot hill and was 28 feet tall. It now serves as a 26-bed dormitory for the marine laboratory of the University of Florida in the Cedar Keys National Wildlife Refuge.

In 1860 Cedar Key became the terminus for the Florida Railroad, and Parson and Hale's General Store was opened in what is now the Island Hotel. Although the town flourished for a time, once the cedar trees had been harvested, the lumber warehouses were converted into shops and restaurants and the town fell into decline.

Things to Do in Cedar Key

A visit to Cedar Key today will reveal a grid of Victorian buildings along the waterfront that now house small shops and fish restaurants. Practical rather than pretty, the waterfront overlooks run-down and weather-beaten fishing huts on stilts out in Waccasassa Bay. The grid of streets that make up the town are lined with simple wooden homes and small gift shops which are interesting to browse.

From the docks there are fishing charters and cruises to offshore island beaches that are ideal for bird-watching within the Cedar Keys National Wildlife Refuge. Back on dry land, the Cedar Key Historical Museum has an eclectic mix of exhibits and is open daily on the corner of D and 2nd Street. However, the very best attraction is taking a seat on the upper deck of one of the restaurants and watching the sun sink down into the Gulf, creating a vibrant sky of rich red, rose, orange and gold in its wake.

Cape San Blas – Off the Beaten Track

What's nice about Cape San Blas is what it is lacking. It has no high-rise condos, no amusement parks, no pollution, no noise and very few people. If you want to enjoy a relaxing break in a place filled with simple pleasures and natural beauty, Cape San Blas is just the place to escape to.

Cape San Blas is on the elbow of the strangely shaped 17-mile long peninsula opposite Port St Joe on the Florida Panhandle. It creates the calm waters of St Joseph Bay, and at the very tip of the spit of land is St Joseph Peninsula State Park.

History of Cape San Blas

Cape San Blas was once an important saltworks, being strategically located in the Gulf of Mexico. This business came to a sudden end when a group of Union soldiers came ashore and destroyed the saltworks in 1862.

Cape San Blas is now on its fourth lighthouse. The first was built in 1847 to warn ships of the dangerous shoals that run out from the Cape. It lacked the necessary height to be seen far out to sea and collapsed in a gale in 1851. A second lighthouse was commissioned, this time built of brick at a cost of $12,000. It was completed in November 1855 and was destroyed the following August by a hurricane. Lighthouse number three was erected in its place in 1858, costing $20,000. It was damaged in 1862 by Union troops during the Civil War and later sea erosion took its toll. In 1883 the present iron-frame lighthouse was constructed. It has an enclosed staircase to the lantern which is 101 feet above sea level.

Things to Do in Cape San Blas

Cape San Blas was named America's #1 beach for its natural beauty in 2002 and when you visit you will understand why. The beaches at Cape San Blas and neighbouring Indian Pass are idyllic with playful surf and white sands scattered with sea shells. The restless sea throws up giant cockles, angel wings, lightning whelks and olive shells that are just begging to be picked up and carried home. The beach is dog-friendly too.

The clear emerald Gulf waters are home to dolphins and some of the best sport fishing in the world. On the north side of the narrow peninsula is St Joseph Bay with calmer waters and more great fishing. Wade out from the shore around Eagle Harbor and you can scoop up scallops by the bucketful. Take them home and steam them for a delicious tasty meal.

Visitors can hit the Peddle Loggerhead Run Bike Trail and ride to Cone Heads then sit and enjoy the rewards of an ice cream. There are a few beach shops and places to eat there. Alternatively you can kayak, take a sailboat out on the bay or book yourself on a snorkeling and diving eco-excursion. Walk along the edge of the waves, spot fiddler crabs, play volleyball with friends or watch the sunset from a swing on the porch. You will definitely want to capture each moment on camera.

Destin – Perfect for Family Vacations

Destin is located in the center of Florida's Panhandle – the long stretch of coast in northwest Florida that runs west from Tallahassee, below the state of Alabama. The beach is overlooked by condos, resorts and skyscrapers along the area known as Holiday Isle, but there are plenty of public beach access points too. Destin harbor is lined with fishing boats of all sizes and nearby there is a great choice of fresh fish and seafood restaurants to suit all budgets.

Getting to Destin is very easy by air into Okaloosa Regional Airport at Fort Walton Beach, just minutes away. Alternatively, Florida's Panhandle coastline is easy to drive to along I-10. If you are driving from Central or South Florida, don't forget to turn your watch back by one hour, as destinations west of Tallahassee are on Central Daylight Time (CDT). The area has over 4 million visitors each year, but it rarely feels crowded, although you may want to make restaurant reservations at weekends.

The resort of Destin is ideal for family vacations with its endless white sandy beaches, warm sea, year-round sunshine and plenty of attractions. It is particularly famous as a sport fishing destination and has been nicknamed "The World's Luckiest Fishing village" due to the record-breaking fish that have been caught here. The Gulf waters are a beautiful sea-green color which has led to the area being known as the "Emerald Coast".

Things to Do in Destin

The region has excellent public golf courses at Fort Walton Beach Golf Club, Golf Garden of Destin, Regatta Bay Golf and Country Club, Seascape Resort and Conference Center and the Emerald Bay Golf Club.

While the boys are out fishing or playing golf, girls can enjoy some retail therapy at one the excellent shopping malls in the area, including the Destin Commons shopping mall and the largest designer outlet center at Silver Sands Outlet Mall. There are plenty of watersports opportunities especially for windsurfing, sailing and parasailing. Destin is a great place to take an unforgettable dolphin cruise to see these friendly creatures racing ahead of the boat's bow or frolicking and playing together.

Still on a water theme, the Destin area has a number of water parks for family fun such as the Pleasure Island Water Park on Fort Walton Beach and the Big Kahuna theme park in Destin. The Gulfarium is home to over 200 marine mammals, fish and reptiles and puts on some excellent dolphin shows.

For days out around Destin consider a trip to Fort Pickens Nature Preserve, part of the Gulf Islands National Seashore on Santa Rosa Island. There is a small admission fee but the area has excellent amenities for fishing, picnicking, shell collecting and walking. It is accessed across the Navarre Bridge off Hwy 98. If you are really lucky you may see an endangered Perdido Key beach mouse or one of the sea turtles that come ashore to lay their eggs in the dunes.

History lovers can take a self-guided tour of the hexagonal-shaped Fort Pickens which dates back to the 1830s, or take a guided tour of Fort Barrancas constructed a few years later. For those with an interest in military history, the nearby US Air Force Armament Museum offers an interesting day out. Hikers can enjoy walks along the Florida Trail which starts at Santa Rosa Island and cyclists can hire bikes and enjoy the five-mile cycle trail on Perdido Key.

With year-round sunshine and average temperatures rarely below 70F even in the winter, Destin is a great place to visit or live in.

Pensacola and the Historic Village

Pensacola is on Florida's Panhandle, so far west it is the last significant city before the border with Alabama. It certainly has a history and culture closer to the Deep South than to the rest of Florida. It even has a different time zone, being one hour behind the majority of Florida.

Pensacola Old City Hall aka Florida State Museum

History of Pensacola

Although visitors to the many beaches along Florida's Panhandle see the area as modern and vibrant with many high-rises and apartment blocks, this area has a long history. Pensacola was where the Spanish first tried to colonize Florida in the mid-16th century and there was plenty of fighting between the Spanish, French, English and Confederates during the next 300 years over who should get the colonial rights.

In 1559 a settlement was established near Pensacola by a party of Spanish colonists led by Tristan de Luna, but it was abandoned just two years later after a hurricane. This makes Pensacola older than the St Augustine community, which remains the oldest continuously occupied settlement in the USA. Pensacola was later re-established but lost out when Tallahassee was chosen as the capital of the New Territory of Florida in the 1820s, being closer to the center of the state.

Historic Pensacola Village

By the 1880s Pensacola was doing very well. The present downtown area was mainly built at this time and had a diverse collection of architectural styles. Wander around Zaragoza Street and Government Street, east of Palafox Place and you will find everything from Colonial cottages to more Classical Revival style homes.

There are excellent walking tours of Historic Pensacola Village with guides in period costume. They run twice daily from Tivoli House on Zaragoza Street and cover the French Creole Lavalle House and the elegant Dorr House. Tickets include the walking tour and entrance to all the properties over two days, so it offers great value for history buffs.

Things to Do in Pensacola

The Civil War Soldiers Museum is fascinating for youngsters as it focuses on the life of ordinary soldiers during the Civil War. It shows the hardships, antique weapons and primitive medical equipment that were around just 150 years ago. In contrast, the Museum of Industry on Tarragona Street brings maritime history to life in relation to Pensacola's thriving timber industry. It has a reconstructed sawmill and a ship's chandlery. Unfortunately, live oaks were very popular for ship building and by the 1930s, most of Florida's mature hardwood forests were gone.

Seek out Fountain Square with its many plaques around a tinkling water feature or sit on a shady park bench in Seville Square, laid out by the British in the 1770s. One of the loveliest buildings is Steamboat House on Government Street, built in the shape of a riverboat, decks and all! In contrast, Pensacola's modern shopping district and malls seem very touristy and anonymous, but they do serve a purpose for shopping and dining in air-conditioned comfort. Pensacola can get very hot and humid in August and September.

The tall black chimney-like Pensacola Lighthouse is still a working lighthouse but is open to visitors. The 172 steep steps are pretty tough and are not suitable for small children, those wearing flip flops, or anyone suffering from vertigo, but the views from the top are superb. Apparently the lighthouse is haunted and some visitors feel the chill and have to leave – so be warned.

Pensacola Beaches

There are some stunningly beautiful sandy beaches close to Pensacola making this a deservedly popular area for family vacations. If you have not experienced the miles of soft white sand and shallow turquoise waters of the Gulf, you have missed out on a visual treat. However, the beaches can get very crowded and noisy and Pensacola Beach is rather touristy. If you want peace and quiet, seek out some of the quieter areas away from Pensacola, such as Fort Pickens, Opal Beach or Perdido Key.

Look out for more books about Florida

by Gillian Birch

- 20 Best Historic Homes in Florida

- Days Out in Central Florida from the Villages

- Favorite Days Out in Central Florida from The Villages' Residents

- Days Out from the Villages with Children

- Days Out Around Orlando

- Days Out Around Fort Myers

- Days Out Around Orlando with Children

These are all available in paperback from your local bookstore and are also available online to download as ebooks

Keep up with future publications at www.gillianbirch.com

ABOUT THE AUTHOR

Gillian Birch is a freelance travel writer and published author. As the wife of a Master Mariner, she has traveled extensively and lived in some exotic locations all over the world including Europe, the Far East and the Republic of Panama. Her love of writing led her to keep detailed journals which are a valuable source of eye-witness information for her many published magazine articles and destination reviews.

Describing herself as having "endless itchy feet and an insatiable wanderlust," she continues to explore Florida and further afield, writing about her experiences with wonderful clarity and attention to detail.

Gillian has a Diploma from the British College of Journalism and is proud to be a member of the International Travel Writers' Alliance and the Gulf Coast Writers' Association. Learn more about her writing as YourTravelGirl at www.gillianbirch.com

Made in the USA
Las Vegas, NV
16 November 2021